FTA-MA-90-5006-02-01
DOT-VNTSC-FTA-02-01

**U.S. Department
of Transportation**

**Federal Transit
Administration**

Handbook for Transit
Safety and Security Certification

Prepared by:
U.S. Department of Transportation
Research and Special Programs Administration
John A. Volpe National Transportation Systems Center
Cambridge, MA 02142-1093

Final Report
November 2002

Prepared for:
Federal Transit Administration
Office of Safety and Security
Washington, DC 20590

FTA OFFICE OF SAFETY AND SECURITY

REPORT DOCUMENTATION PAGE

Form Approved
OMB No. 0704-0188

Public reporting burden for this collection of information is estimated to average 1 hour per response, including the time for reviewing instructions, searching existing data sources, gathering and maintaining the data needed, and completing and reviewing the collection of information. Send comments regarding this burden estimate or any other aspect of this collection of information, including suggestions for reducing this burden, to Washington Headquarters Services, Directorate for Information Operations and Reports, 1215 Jefferson Davis Highway, Suite 1204, Arlington, VA 22202-4302, and to the Office of Management and Budget, Paperwork Reduction Project (0704-0188), Washington, DC 20503.

1. AGENCY USE ONLY (Leave blank)	2. REPORT DATE November 2002	3. REPORT TYPE AND DATES COVERED Final Report September 2000 – November 2002

4. TITLE AND SUBTITLE

Handbook for Transit Safety and Security Certification

6. AUTHOR(S)

Robert J. Adduci, Annabelle Boyd, and Jim Caton

5. FUNDING NUMBERS

U2169/TM20A

7. PERFORMING ORGANIZATION NAME(S) AND ADDRESS(ES)

U.S. Department of Transportation
Research and Special Programs Administration
Volpe National Transportation Systems Center
55 Broadway, Kendall Square
Cambridge, MA 02142-1093

8. PERFORMING ORGANIZATION REPORT NUMBER

DOT-VNTSC-FTA-02-01

9. SPONSORING/MONITORING AGENCY NAME(S) AND ADDRESS(ES)

U.S. Department of Transportation
Federal Transit Administration
Office of Program Management,
Office of Safety and Security
Washington, DC 20590

10. SPONSORING/MONITORING AGENCY REPORT NUMBER

DOT-FTA-MA-90-5006-02-01

11. SUPPLEMENTARY NOTES

12a. DISTRIBUTION/AVAILABILITY STATEMENT

This document is available to the public through the National Technical Information Service, Springfield, VA 22161

12b. DISTRIBUTION CODE

13. ABSTRACT (Maximum 200 words)

The Joint Task Force on Safety and Security Certification, established between the Federal Transit Administration (FTA) and the American Public Transportation Association (APTA), prepared this Handbook to support the efforts of the transit industry to achieve continuous improvement in safety and security performance. This Handbook provides a guide for establishing a certification program to address safety and security that identifies the key activities; incorporates safety and security more fully into transit projects; highlights resources necessary to develop and implement a certification program for safety and security; and provides tools and sample forms to promote implementation of the safety and security certification process.

14. SUBJECT TERMS

System safety; system security; safety certification; verification

15. NUMBER OF PAGES

54

16. PRICE CODE

17. SECURITY CLASSIFICATION OF REPORT	18. SECURITY CLASSIFICATION OF THIS PAGE	19. SECURITY CLASSIFICATION OF ABSTRACT	20. LIMITATION OF ABSTRACT
Unclassified	Unclassified	Unclassified	

NSN 7540-01-280-5500

Standard Form 298 (Rev. 2-89)
Prescribed by ANSI Std. 239-18

Foreword

The *Joint Task Force on Safety and Security Certification*, established between the Federal Transit Administration (FTA) and the American Public Transportation Association (APTA), prepared this Handbook to support the efforts of the transit industry to achieve continuous improvement in safety and security performance.

Federal Transit Administration Online Resources

Office of Safety and Security   http://www.fta.dot.gov (click on "Safety and Security)

National Transit Library: http://www.fta.dot.gov/ntl/index/html

Planning	http://www.fta.dot.gov/ntl/planning/index.html
Best Practices	http://www.fta.dot.gov/ntl/bestpractices/index.html
Procurement	http://www.fta.dot.gov/ntl/procurement/index.html
Policy	http://www.fta.dot.gov/ntl/policy/index.html

The practice described in this Handbook is the result of a year-long research and consensus-building mission, that included the review of dozens of industry programs and plans; the collection of issue-specific information from transit safety and security directors, project managers, contractors, operations personnel, and FTA Regional Offices; presentations and working sessions with industry representatives; and requests to industry for review and comment on draft materials.

This Handbook provides a guide for establishing a certification program to address safety and security that:

- Identifies the key activities

- Incorporates safety and security more fully into transit projects

- Highlights resources necessary to develop and implement a certification program for safety and security

American Public Transportation Association Online Resources

APTA recently added the "Transit Safety Corner" – an ongoing source of information on safety issues critical to the public transportation industry—to its web site. You can access APTA's Safety Corner at:

http://www.apta.com/services/safety/index.htm

The site also offers a Question and Answer section that is available to the industry. The site is designed to address questions that are of concern to a particular agency. The responses are generated automatically to any individual who has requested their name be placed on APTA's 'list server.' The list server is made up on individuals from various agencies that have agreed to become part of this process. If you would like to be placed on the 'list server' write to the Safety and Security section at www.apta.com.

- Provides tools and sample forms to promote implementation of the safety and security certification process

This Handbook is not intended to be prescriptive in nature. Rather, information can be tailored to suit the individual needs of transit projects. The transit agencies are responsible for determining applicability of these concepts to their own projects or developing other workable processes. Differences in methodology may exist among transit agencies, as well as among projects within a single transit agency.

Joint FTA-APTA Task Force on Safety and Security Certification
Harry Saporta, Chairman
Federal Transit Administration, Office of Safety and Security

Bill Grizard, Vice-Chairman
American Public Transportation Association

Bob Adduci, Volpe National Transportation Systems Center
Don Dzinski, Egis, Inc.
Howard Fegles, Oregon Department of Transportation
Roy Field, Federal Transit Administration, Office of Safety and Security
Fred Goodine, Washington Metropolitan Area Transit Authority
Greg Hull, American Public Transportation Association
Linda Meadow, Linda J. Meadow & Associates
Conrad Santana, Siemens, Tren Urbano
Bob Sedlock, New Jersey Department of Transportation
Maria Taylor, American Public Transportation Association

Supporting Members -- The following individuals contributed generously of their time and materials in preparation of this Handbook:

SAFETY:
Harvey Becker, San Francisco Municipal Railway
Luke Chisenhall, Dallas Area Rapid Transit
Jack Collins, Santa Clara Valley Transportation Authority
Michael Conlon, Metropolitan Council, Hiawatha Light Rail
Tom Eng, Los Angeles Metropolitan Transportation Authority
Jack Graham, Dallas Area Rapid Transit
Len Hardy, Bay Area Rapid Transit
Hugh Johnson, Utah Transit Authority
Pamela McCombe, Greater Cleveland Regional Transit Authority
Henry Miranda, Bay Area Rapid Transit
Brian Moriarty, TRW
Laura Smith, New York Metropolitan Transportation Authority
Nagal Shashidhara, Hudson-Bergen Light Rail
Nancy Shea, Massachusetts Bay Transportation Authority
Roger Wood, GMAEC-DMJM, Tren Urbano

SECURITY:
Dan Cowden, Los Angeles County Metropolitan Transportation Authority
Paul Lennon. Los Angeles County Metropolitan Transportation Authority
Clark Lynch, Bay Area Rapid Transit
Joe McKinney, Metropolitan Atlanta Regional Transportation Authority
David Scott, Southeastern Pennsylvania Transportation Authority

STATE SAFETY OVERSIGHT:
Brian Cristy, Massachusetts Department of Telecommunications and Energy
Ray Jantzen, Colorado Public Utilities Commission
Robert Strauss, California Public Utilities Commission
Bob Kraus, Missouri Department of Economic Development

Technical Support -- Annabelle Boyd and James Caton, of the BCG Transportation Group, Inc. supported the development and documentation of Task Force research, findings and recommendations in this Handbook.

Table of Contents

List of Figures

Acknowledgments

The Task Force is extremely grateful for the contributions made to this Handbook from its safety and security partners in industry and State government:

Four new start systems, Utah Transit Authority (UTA) Transit Express Rail System (TRAX), New Jersey Transit's (NJT) Hudson-Bergen Light Rail Transit (HBLRT) System, Metropolitan Council's Hiawatha Light Rail Line (Metro Transit), and the Government of Puerto Rico, Department Transportation and Public Works, Highway and Transportation Authority (Tren Urbano) provided their programs for addressing unique safety and security certification challenges during the major capital project development process.

San Francisco Municipal Railway (MUNI) offered its policies and safety design criteria for integrating an entirely new line – its Third Street Rail Project – into its existing operations. Dallas Area Rapid Transit (DART), San Francisco Bay Area Rapid Transit District (BART), Washington Metropolitan Area Transit Authority (WMATA), Tri-County Metropolitan Transit District of Oregon (Tri-Met), the Los Angeles County Metropolitan Transportation Authority (LACMTA), and the Santa Clara Valley Transportation Authority (VTA) all provided their programs for planning, designing, and integrating major extensions into operations.

St. Louis Bi-State Development Agency (Bi-State) shared its program for conducting hazard analysis during extension design and engineering, and tracking the resolution of identified hazards through testing and acceptance. The Massachusetts Bay Transit Authority (MBTA) and APTA have contributed safety certification programs that support basic procurement processes, even when no major acquisition project is underway.

Finally, several State Safety Oversight Agencies have contributed their program requirements and standards for rail transit design and construction, including New Jersey Department of Transportation (NJDOT), Utah Department of Transportation (UDOT), the Oregon Department of Transportation (ODOT), the Massachusetts Department of Telecommunications and Energy (DTE), the Missouri Department of Economic Development, Division of Motor Carrier and Railroad Safety (MCRS), the Colorado Public Utilities Commission (CoPUC), and the California Public Utilities Commission (CPUC).

Organization

To support implementation of practices that result in the design and construction of transit projects that maximize safety and security performance within available resources, the Federal Transit Administration (FTA), through its Joint Task Force on Safety and Security Certification, has prepared this Handbook. The procedures described in this Handbook enable transit management, the project team, and all others involved in the project, to address safety and security requirements in a consistent and dedicated program, throughout the development process.

This Handbook is organized in two chapters:

> Chapter 1 – The Basics: Introduces the basic concepts of certification for safety and security, and explains why, since its development only a few short decades ago, this type of certification has become an integral part of effective project management practice.

> Chapter 2 – The Tools: Introduces three tools that support the safety and security certification process:

> - *Well-defined project scope* – to establish applicability of the certification program for project elements and to encourage shared vision among the project team

> - *Safety and Security Certification Plan* – to establish roles and responsibilities for the certification process and to define key activities

> - *10-step Safety and Security Certification Methodology* – to provide a consistent process for verifying safety and security requirements throughout all phases of project activity

> Chapter 2 also provides sample forms to support implementation of the certification program.

Appendices offer additional information on key topics discussed in the Handbook, including:

> Appendix A: Project Life Cycle Definitions
> Appendix B: Useful Safety and Security Certification Resources
> Appendix C: Resource Guide
> Appendix D: Sample Design and Construction Specification Form and Directions

This Handbook should provide each member of the project team with a basic understanding of the certification practice, demonstrating the importance of each technical and managerial discipline to the overall safety and security mission.

Chapter 1
The Basics

As used in this Handbook, certification for safety and security is defined as:

> the series of processes that collectively verify the safety and security readiness of a project for public use.

While this Handbook emphasizes rail transit projects – including both "new start" systems and extensions to existing systems – its principles and practices extend to major projects for all modes, including bus transit.

Depending on project scope and resources, the process described in this Handbook should be tailored to an appropriate level of specificity, determined by the agency.

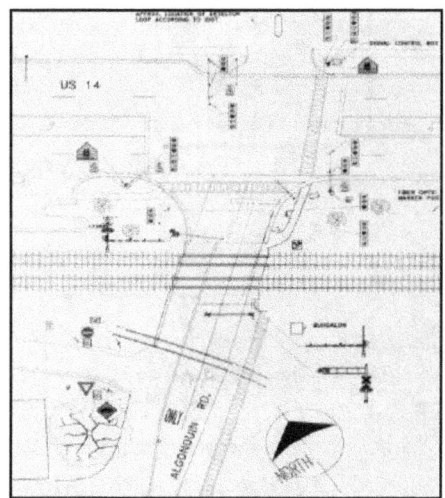

Certification, as used in this Handbook, addresses conditions that could result in harm – whether unintentional (safety) or intentional (security). Application of safety and security certification promotes an informed management decision-making process in project design, construction, testing, and initiation into revenue service.

CERTIFICATION AS PART OF SYSTEM SAFETY AND SECURITY

The system safety and security discipline manages hazards and vulnerabilities throughout the life cycle of a project, program, or activity through a committed approach to risk management, where:

> ➤ a <u>hazard</u> is a condition or circumstance that could lead to an unplanned or undesired event;
>
> ➤ a <u>vulnerability</u> is a characteristic of the system that increases the probability of occurrence of a security incident; and
>
> ➤ <u>risk</u> is an expression of the impact of an undesired event or security incident in terms of severity and likelihood.

Certification for safety and security verifies application of this discipline for transit projects. Through this process, hazards and vulnerabilities are translated into risks, which are then analyzed, assessed, prioritized, and resolved, accepted, or tracked. Figure 1 presents this process as a continuous loop, providing for validation of decisions and on-going evaluation to support further action. This process supports the consideration of safety and security objectives during all activities of the dynamic and evolving project management process.

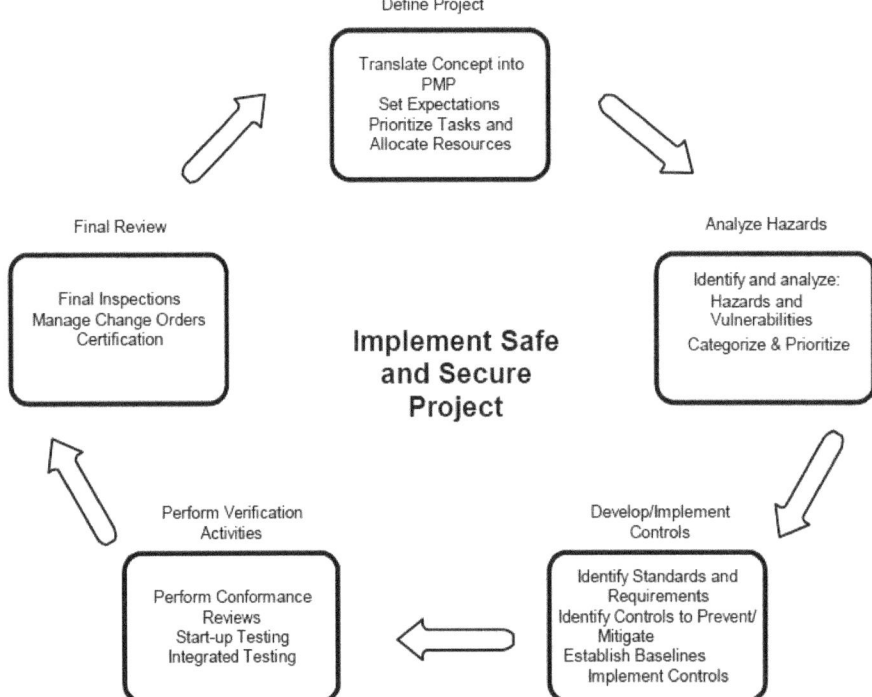

Figure 1: Safety and Security Core Management Functions

Certification for safety and security is **NOT** contractual acceptance, defined as:

> an action by an authorized representative of the transit agency by which the transit agency assumes full or partial ownership of the delivered project as complete or partial performance of a contract.

Contractual acceptance does not constitute safety and security certification, and safety and security certification need not imply acceptance with respect to contract performance.

SAFETY AND SECURITY CERTIFICATION BENEFITS

Many transit agencies self-certify the safety and security of their operations, subsequent extensions and safety-significant modifications, prior to the initiation of revenue service. This process is typically part of the agency's existing program for system safety and security, and is integrated into major projects through a Safety and Security Certification (SSC) Program, documented in a Safety and Security Certification Plan (SSCP).

In certain instances, transit agencies have received benefits from the SSC during engineering and design. SSC activities support analysis that reduces the need for expensive retrofitting to correct hazards or vulnerabilities after the system is placed in revenue service. Certification also typically supports improved integration of operational considerations into project design, which offers the following opportunities:

- Improved functionality of system design
- Promotion of effective and efficient use of resources
- Reduction in work-arounds and change orders during construction
- Reduction in hazards in service and maintenance activities

In the event that accidents or major security incidents do occur, certification offers the following benefits, which may be useful in legal and insurance proceedings:

- Hazards and vulnerabilities are identified and assessed, and documented action is taken to resolve identified critical and catastrophic hazards as soon as possible.

- Appropriate codes, guidelines, and standards are reviewed to provide a basis for safety and security consideration in the design criteria and specifications, and drawings are in conformance with the design criteria.

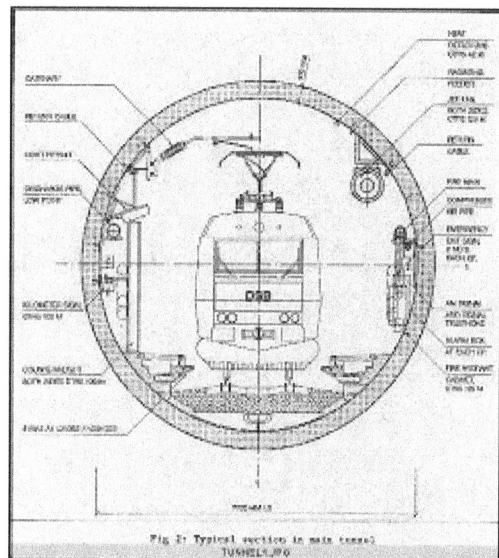

- Facilities, systems, and equipment are designed, constructed, built, inspected, and tested in accordance with applicable codes, standards, criteria, and specifications.

- Necessary verification tests, safety plans, security plans, operating procedures, and rule books are developed for operations.

- Personnel are trained and qualified to respond to emergencies, and emergency response organizations are familiar with the transit systems and its emergency procedures.

TRANSIT AGENCY COMMITMENT

The self-certification that guides each agency's SSC process reflects that agency's commitment to verify that its operation is free from unacceptable risk. This is a proactive approach to safety and security with clear objectives to identify, anticipate, and control adverse conditions before they occur. Through SSC, each transit agency typically makes a commitment to:

- **Develop a policy formalizing management risk acceptance practices** for activities that affect the safety and security of the operational system
- **Identify and document the safety- and security-critical elements** that comprise the project
- **Specify and apply safety and security requirements**, consistent with approved risk management practices, to these elements, through the use of design criteria, design manuals, contract specifications, and safety and security analysis
- **Implement a dedicated program of hazard and vulnerability analysis and tracking**, which verifies, for each safety- and security-critical element, the identification, evaluation, and resolution of all conditions with the potential to result in death, severe injury, multiple injury, system loss, major system damage, or major environmental impact
- **Implement a dedicated program of review** to verify that safety and security requirements are included in specifications, test plans, procedures, and operational assessments for the project, and coordinated with all transit departments that have responsibilities for the project
- **Implement a dedicated program of testing and evaluation**, to verify that safety- and security-critical elements, delivered to the agency, comply with contract specifications, and that an acceptable level of operational readiness and emergency preparedness exists among the transit departments and personnel responsible for initiating the project into revenue service
- **Issue written Certificates of Compliance** (COC) for each safety- and security-critical element, indicating that it meets established safety and security requirements
- **Issue Project Safety and Security Certificate**, along with a Final Verification Report, verifying the project's readiness for safe and secure revenue service.

RESPONSIBILITY FOR SSC PROGRAM

Ultimate responsibility for the development and operation of a safe and secure system rests with the transit agency's executive leadership. The transit agency provides direction and guidance for the safety and security certification program. During project development, implementation of the SSC program is often delegated to the project management team, which verifies performance of all certification tasks.

In existing transit systems, certification for safety and security is often managed by the safety and/or security manager (Certification Manager). For agencies with New Start projects, the staggered approach required to support project development brings many different participants with varying levels of responsibility over a period of several years. In this environment, the SSC program should provide a consistent focus on safety and security for all activities. This Handbook also uses the term "Certification Manager" to address the range of personnel who may manage this process.

COMMITTEE INVOLVEMENT

Several safety and security committees, including the following, may support the SSC program. In a transit agency, the functions described below may be combined, or may be performed by individuals rather than committees.

Safety and Security Review Committee (SRC): Many transit agencies have found it beneficial to create a Safety and Security Review Committee -- or equivalent multi-disciplinary group -- to oversee the conduct of safety and security efforts for the project, directly accountable to the transit agency's executive leadership. The SRC is typically chaired by a full-time System Safety and/or Security Manager or the Certification Manager. The SRC is typically comprised of senior management personnel, or their designees, who represent the major project areas and activities. The SRC oversees the SSC program and directs resolution of identified hazards. The SRC discusses ongoing safety and security concerns; reviews and approves certification activities; and resolves issues among the project team and with the agency's executive leadership.

Fire-Life Safety Committee (FLSC). This Committee is to serve as a liaison between the transit agency, fire jurisdictions, and emergency response agencies. The FLSC may be comprised of local and state fire jurisdictions, local emergency response agencies, transit operations, safety, security, construction and design managers, along with transit management staff and the general design consultant. The FLSC reviews standards and safety-related designs and tests to verify fire-life safety code and regulation compliance. In addition, the FLSC addresses preparedness issues and reviews variances.

System Change and Operations Review Committee (SCORC). This Committee's responsibilities include planning and coordinating operational training, simulating revenue service conditions, and developing pre-revenue plans, rules, and procedures for revenue service. Prior to revenue service, the SCORC reviews procedures, manuals, and other documents that form the basis for certifying compliance to safety and security requirements for systems and fixed facilities. The SCORC may also be responsible for review and concurrence of proposed changes and/or revisions to the project design.

APPLICATION OF THE PROJECT LIFE CYCLE

Many transit agencies use a standard life cycle framework to manage transit projects, such as the one shown in Figure 2 below. This life cycle defines the events, procedures and tasks that take place within the project. Each life cycle phase may conclude with a review, enabling management evaluation. Appendix A provides a brief description of activities typically performed in each life cycle phase.

Advancement through this process is based on a project's readiness to progress to subsequent phases. Transition from one life cycle phase to the next phase constitutes a MILESTONE CONTROL for all major project elements, including safety and security.

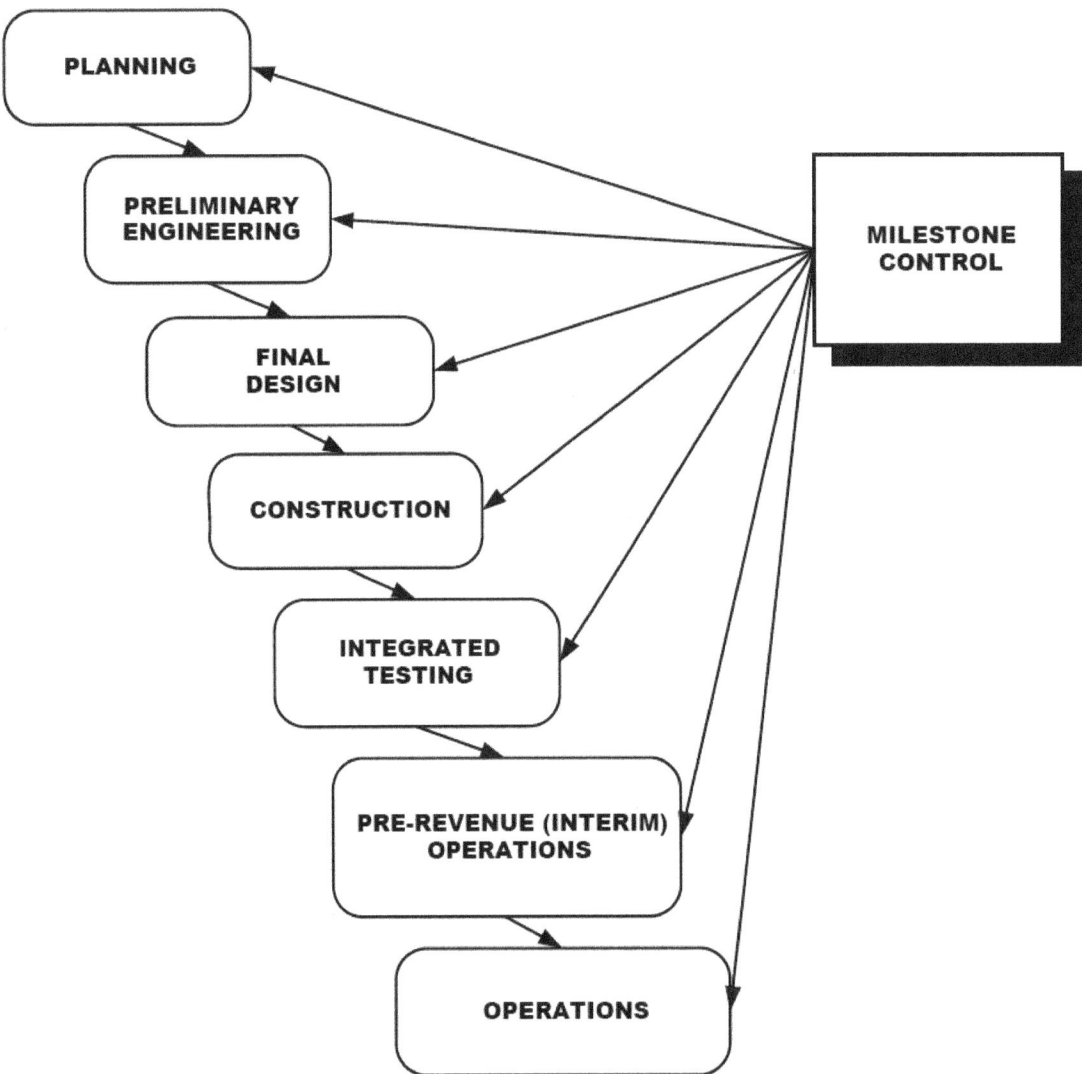

Figure 2: Typical Transit Project Life Cycle

SAMPLE ACTIVITIES

A sample listing of typical activities performed during the certification process is presented in Figure 3, below. Figure 3 categorizes key activities for each of the project life cycle phases:

> PLN – Planning
> PE – Preliminary Engineering
> FD – Final Design
> CON – Construction
> INT-TEST – Integrated Testing
> PRE-REV – Pre-revenue (Interim) Operations
> OPS – Operations

Checks (✓) indicate the initiation of the activity, and shaded arrows (▶▶) indicate ongoing performance.

In managing these activities, Certification Managers typically work closely with the project team to address the following:

- Roles and responsibilities for safety and security (at all levels of the organization)

- Required resources and project schedule for safety and security activities

- Procedures and programs to ensure safety and security integration into design, construction, testing and acceptance, and start-up activities

- The process for the identification and effective communication of safety hazards and security vulnerabilities associated with the operational phase of the transit project

- The process for sound decision-making which integrates the results of system safety and security activities into the requirements and specifications for the project

Figure 3 is a representative sample only. The scope of each project should be considered to determine the tasks that are appropriate.

TASK	PLN	PE	FD	CON	INT-TEST	PRE-REV	OPS
Develop Safety and Security Policy	✓	»»	»»	»»	»»	»»	»»
Assign SSC Responsibilities	✓	»»	»»	»»	»»	»»	»»
Establish Safety and Security Committees	✓	»»	»»	»»	»»	»»	»»
Identify Existing Safety and Security Requirements for Acquisition Process	✓	»»	»»	»»	»»	»»	»»
Develop Safety and Security Certification Plan		✓	»»	»»	»»	»»	»»
Identify Safety and Security Certifiable Elements & Items		✓	»»	»»	»»	»»	»»
Initiate Project Documentation System		✓	»»	»»	»»	»»	»»
Perform Preliminary Hazard and Vulnerability Analysis		✓	»»	»»	»»	»»	»»
Prepare Safety and Security Design Criteria		✓	»»	»»	»»	»»	»»
Integrate Operations and Maintenance Requirements into Design		✓	»»	»»	»»	»»	»»
Develop Design Criteria Conformance Checklists		✓	»»	»»	»»	»»	»»
Perform Safety and Security Design Reviews			✓	»»	»»	»»	»»
Perform Additional Hazard and Vulnerability Analyses (as applicable)			✓	»»	»»	»»	»»
Implement Hazard and Vulnerability Resolution and Tracking			✓	»»	»»	»»	»»
Verify Design Criteria Conformance Checklists			✓	»»	»»	»»	»»
Identify Safety and Security Requirements for Test Program Plans, Integrated Testing and Operational Readiness			✓	»»	»»	»»	»»
Develop Specification Conformance Checklists (Construction)			✓	»»	»»	»»	»»
Complete Specification Conformance Checklists				✓	»»	»»	»»
Issue Permits and Certificates (as applicable)				✓	»»	»»	»»
Complete Integrated Tests					✓	»»	»»
Safety and Security Review of Engineering Change Orders & Waivers						✓	»»
Complete Operations & Maintenance Plans, Procedures and Training						✓	»»
Complete Operational Readiness Review (including work-arounds)						✓	»»
Issue Final Safety and Security Certification						✓	»»
Issue Final Safety and Security Verification Report						✓	»»

Figure 3: Project Development Safety and Security Activities

PROJECT TEAM SUPPORT FOR THE SSC

Each member of the project team has a role in safety and security certification. While the Certification Manager has primary responsibility for SSC management, the tasks required to perform the SSC include many functional disciplines on the project team. As indicated in Figure 4 below, the Certification Manager should support a coordinated effort that brings the capabilities and resources of the design team, the construction team, the acceptance and testing team, and the activation team to the performance of SSC activities.

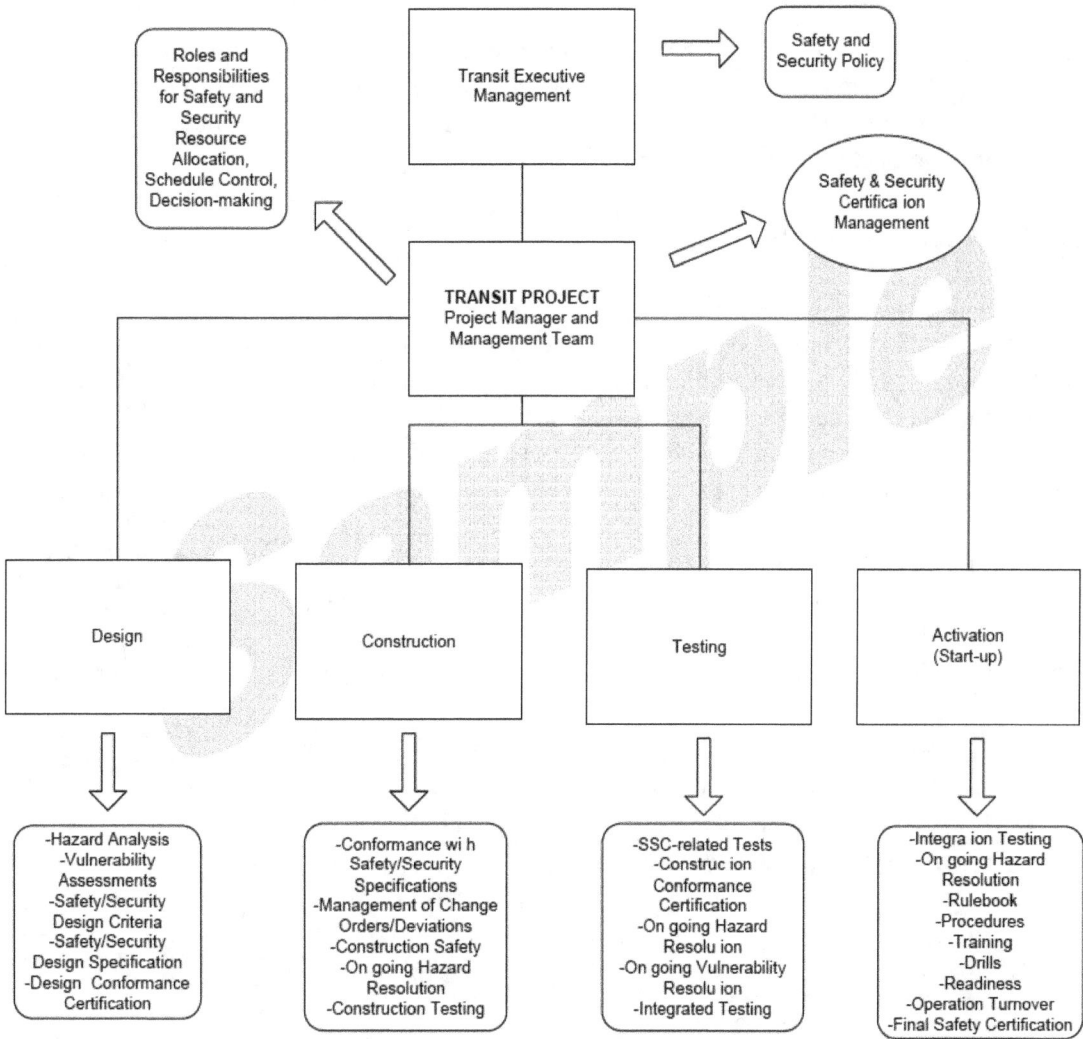

Figure 4: Contributions of Project Team to SSC

MANAGING DOCUMENTATION

To manage the SSC program, a documentation system is strongly recommended. This system may contain documents pertaining to the certification process. The project filing system may fulfill this requirement, or may be supported by an additional system.

In general, safety and security certification documentation should be maintained for the life of the agency. Security information and other sensitive information should be protected using agency policies and procedures.

An important part of the safety certification process is keeping transit management informed of the status of the program. To ensure that executive leadership is informed, periodic reports are prepared. The reporting period may change from time to time, dependent upon activity levels and project priorities.

SAFETY AUDIT PROGRAM

Throughout the verification effort, audits should be conducted on a periodic basis, by a management team independent of the program. Audits should verify that all participants in the design conformance and testing/acceptance processes are reviewing compliance with safety and security requirements and appropriately documenting this conformance. Other activities to be assessed include the following:

- The status of each safety task
- Compliance with program milestones and safety program milestones
- Schedule incompatibilities that require remedial corrective action
- Action to track and implement positive corrective actions where deficiencies are revealed
- Project team activity to support the SSC program
- Configuration management

tech tip

Linked worksheets, supported in a database, can reduce document preparation time and promote consistency from project phase to project phase.

Chapter 2
The Tools

SCOPE OF THE SSC PROGRAM

The SSC program typically encompasses the equipment, operating and maintenance plans, facilities, and procedures for the following three categories:

- **Systemwide Elements** – may include the passenger vehicles, catenary, traction power, train control system, voice and data communications, CCTV, grade crossing and traffic control system, intrusion detection system, traction power substations, central instrument houses, track, fare collection, supervisory control, fire protection and suppression systems, and auxiliary vehicles and equipment.

- **Fixed Facilities** – may include stations and shelter stops, pedestrian bridges, yard and shop, structures, and the control center. Equipment installed in stations or shelter stops such as HVAC, escalators, elevators is also considered part of the facility.

- **Plans, Procedures, and Training** – may include items such as emergency preparedness plans, security plans and procedures, training programs, rule books, and standard operating procedures.

When properly scoped, the SSC program will:

- Develop, document, and communicate safety and security criteria to guide design, engineering, and specification for the transit project

- Identify safety and security critical issues and develop practical and cost-effective requirements to support their resolution

- Use hazard and vulnerability analysis to evaluate the impacts of all deviations introduced into the system in the form of engineering change proposals, construction change orders, work-arounds and other temporary measures prior to the initiation of revenue service

- Develop management mechanisms to track and control the incorporation of safety and security into the transit project.

SAFETY AND SECURITY CERTIFICATION PLAN

The Safety and Security Certification Plan is a basic tool used by the transit organization to assist in managing an effective certification program. The SSCP provides the formal basis of understanding and agreement among all members of the project team regarding how the program will be executed. The SSCP typically describes the process through which the transit agency activity will provide documented verification that:

- A certifiable elements list is developed

- Safety and security design criteria are developed to identify concerns appropriate for the project

- A design checklist is developed and completed to verify compliance of contract specifications with the safety and security criteria

- Construction checklists are developed and completed to verify that facilities and systems are constructed, manufactured or installed according to design

- Integrated tests are identified that need to be monitored for safety and security

- Training classes are provided to transit operations and maintenance staff that address safety, security, and emergency preparedness

- Operations and maintenance manuals are provided to, or developed by, transit operations and maintenance staff

- Operations and maintenance staff are trained on rules and procedures.

- Public safety personnel (i.e., fire and police) are trained to manage their activities safely in the transit environment

- Emergency drills are conducted for identified transit emergencies that may occur on the project

- Hazard and vulnerability identification and resolution are performed with tracking for resolution and/or acceptance throughout the project

- The "Certificate of Safety and Security" is issued to verify that the transit project is safe and secure for revenue service

- The Safety Certification Verification Report is prepared, and transmitted, as appropriate to management and oversight personnel

- The transit project successfully complies with identified safety and security requirements.

A typical *Table of Contents* for the SSCP follows:

SSCP SAMPLE TABLE OF CONTENTS

===

Section 1: Introduction

- Authority
- Introduction
- Purpose
- Objectives
- Definition
- Responsibility
- Scope
- Certification Revisions

Section 2: Program Management

- Project Team
- Safety and Security Review Committee
- Fire/Life Safety Committee
- System Change and Operations Review Committee

Section 3: Certification Process and Procedures

- General
- Certifiable Elements
- Criteria Conformance Checklist
- Specification Conformance and Operational Readiness Checklists
- Tests & Inspections
- Integrated Testing and Integrated Test Permit

- Plans and Procedures
- Training Programs
- Emergency Drills

Section 4: Hazard and Vulnerability Management

- General
- Responsibility
- Hazard Identification and Analysis
- Threat and Vulnerability Assessment
- Resolution Process
- Open Items List

Section 5: Certificate of Conformance

- Issuance
- Exceptions

Section 6: Documentation

- Requirements
- Responsibilities

Section 7: Reporting Requirements

- Periodic Reports
- Final Certification
- Final Verification Report

STEPS IN THE SSC METHODOLOGY

The remainder of this Handbook explains the SSC methodology, providing a brief a description of each step, and presenting sample forms to support the certification process. Appendices B and C provide additional references for further information on certification activities. Appendix D provides a sample Design and Construction Specification Form and directions for completion.

The following steps typically comprise the SSC methodology:

Step 1: Identify Certifiable Elements
Step 2: Develop Safety and Security Design Criteria
Step 3: Develop and Complete Design Criteria Conformance Checklist
Step 4: Perform Construction Specification Conformance
Step 5: Identify Additional Safety and Security Test Requirements
Step 6: Perform Testing and Validation in Support of the SSC Program
Step 7: Manage Integrated Tests for the SSC Program
Step 8: Manage "Open Items" in the SSC Program
Step 9: Verify Operational Readiness
Step 10: Conduct Final Determination of Project Readiness and Issue Safety and Security Certification

STEP 1: Identify Certifiable Elements

The first step in the SSC methodology is to identify the elements that need to be certified for the transit project. Safety certifiable elements include all project elements that can affect the safety and security of transit agency passengers, employees, contractors, emergency responders, or the general public. These elements define the scope of the project's certification program. Prior to the initiation of revenue service, a Certificate of Compliance will need to be issued for each identified element.

Certifiable elements are composed of numerous items. These items make up the whole of the major element and require individual safety and security verification before the major element is verified as safe and secure for use. The listing of these items for a major element is typically referred to as a Certifiable Item List (CIL).

The process of "breaking down" certifiable elements into CILs typically occurs simultaneously with the project team's engineering effort. As depicted in Figure 5, the engineering breakdown structure supports identification of CILs for each certifiable element – particularly for complex systems (train control upgrades, new vehicles) and projects with a significant emphasis on integration into an existing operation.

Specific certifiable items on the list are dependent on the particular element. In addition, listing of a certifiable item may need to be duplicated a number of times within a certifiable element. For example, each light rail vehicle requires individual verification, and each is tracked as a sub-element of the element "Light Rail Vehicle." Similarly, there are a number of duplicate certifiable items for train signals, traction power, track, and other elements. Each element may also be divided into sub-elements equivalent to a particular section of the alignment of the light rail system being verified.

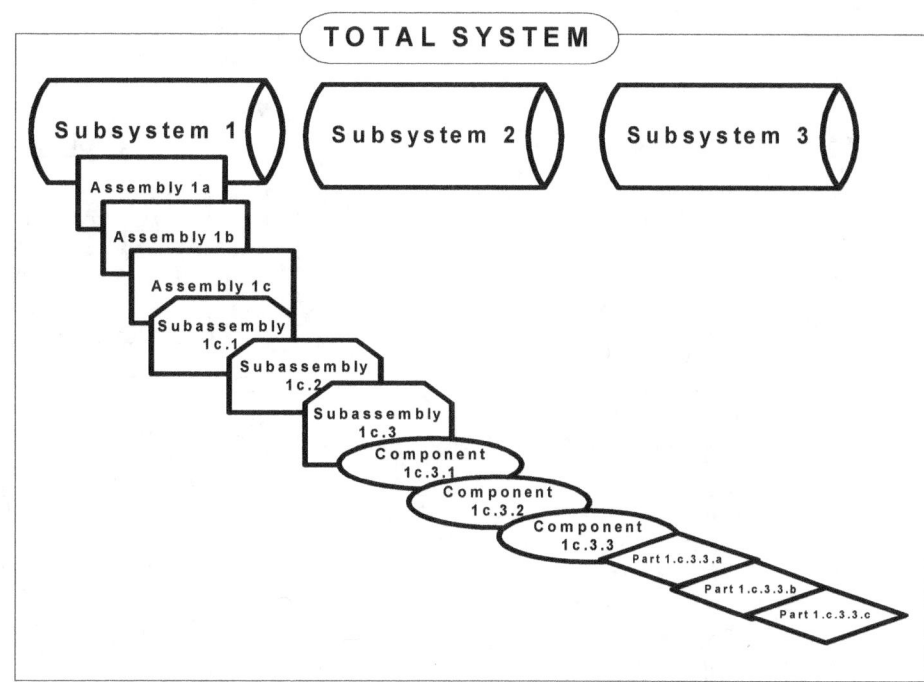

Figure 5: Engineering Breakdown Structure

Figure 6 presents major groupings of certifiable elements and sub-elements for a rail transit project. This is a sample listing provided for illustrative purposes only. Each agency must determine those elements requiring safety and security certification based on its own policies and the scope of the project.

SAMPLE CERIFIABLE ELEMENTS AND SUB-ELEMENTS LIST	
SYSTEMS	**CIVIL INSTALLATIONS**

SYSTEMS

VEHICLE

- Carbody
- Coupler
- Doors, Door Operators and Controls
- Trucks and Suspension
- Propulsion
- Braking
- Operator's Cab and Controls
- Communication Equipment
- Mobility Lift
- Lighting
- HVAC
- Fire/Flammability/Smoke Emissions

SIGNALS

- Interlocking Circuits/Equipment
- Mainline Controls and Indications
- Grade Crossing Warning Devices
- Yard/Mainline Interface
- Track Signals
- LRT Signals
- Signal Indications
- Train Protection

COMMUNICATIONS

- Radio System
- Operations Control Center
- SCADA
- Fire Department Communications
- Security Communications
- Security Systems
- Fire Systems
- Public Address Systems

TRACTION POWER SYSTEMS

- Enclosures
- High Voltage Switchgear
- AC to DC Conversion
- DC Switchgear
- Batteries and Accessories
- Catenary
- Stray Current Protection

CIVIL INSTALLATIONS

TRACK AND STRUCTURES

- Right of Way
- Track
- Aerial
- At-grade
- Underground
- Barriers and Warnings

YARD AND SHOP

- Electrical Safety Provisions
- Vehicle Movement Provisions
- Track and Appliances
- Building (Occupancy)
- Fire System
- Lifts/Elevator

STATIONS/PARKING LOTS

- Platforms
- Handicapped Access Provisions
- Elevators and Escalators
- Illumination
- Electrical Grounding

SIGNAGE

PROCURED ITEMS

TRAFFIC SIGNAL CONTROLLERS
MOBILITY IMPAIRED LIFTS
TRACTION POWER SUBSTATIONS
TICKET VENDING EQUIPMENT

PLANS, PROCEDURES AND TRAINING

TEST PLANS

- Acceptance Tests
- Integrated Tests
- Pre-Revenue Tests

OPERATING AND MAINTENANCE PROGRAM
- Standard Operating Procedures (SOPs)
- Emergency Operating Procedures (EOPs)
- Manuals and Rulebooks
- Training and Certification (if applicable)
- Local Responder Training
- Emergency Preparedness

Figure 6: Sample Certifiable Elements and Sub-elements List

Figure 7 illustrates how certifiable elements are addressed in the project. At each stage of the process, for each certifiable element, conformance with project safety and security requirements is verified; certified through issuance of certificates prior to revenue service; and documented in a Final Verification Report.

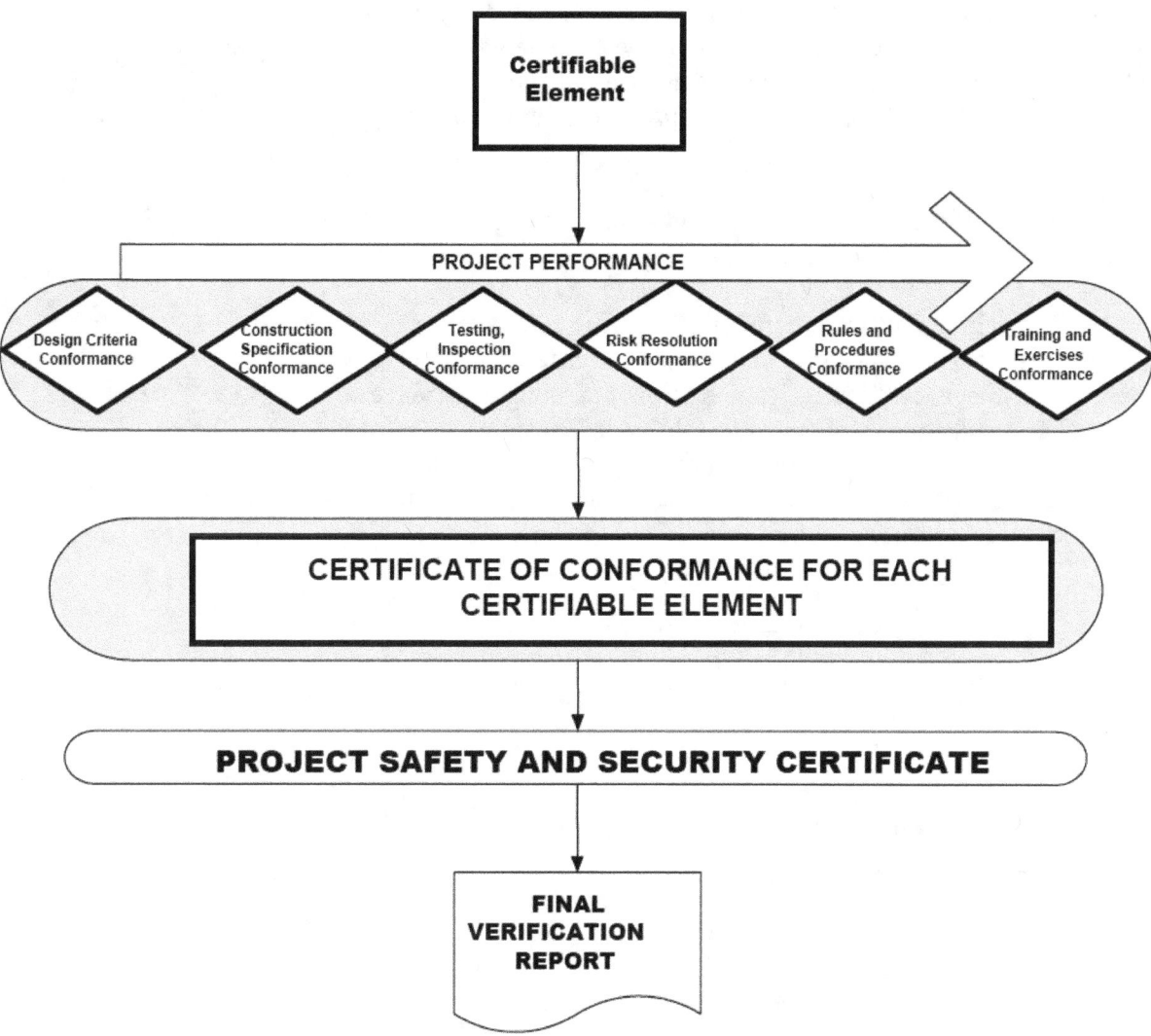

Figure 7: Certifiable Elements and the Certification Process

STEP 2: Develop Safety and Security Design Criteria

Design is an iterative process. Safety and security are addressed during project design through identification of safety and security design criteria for each certifiable element. Safety and security design criteria are intended to provide guidance to the design team to support the definition of systems, sub-systems and components, the development of performance requirements, and the final specification of the engineered system. Whenever possible, reference to their identification and documentation should be included in the procurement package for design services.

As indicated in Figure 8 below, safety and security design criteria are often generated from:

1. The technical specifications from previous contracts
2. Existing agency design and performance criteria
3. Transit agency "lessons learned" from operating experience
4. The results of hazard and vulnerability analysis
5. Transit industry safety and security practice and reports
6. Applicable safety and security codes, standards, and regulations defined by Federal, state and local agencies and standards boards and organizations

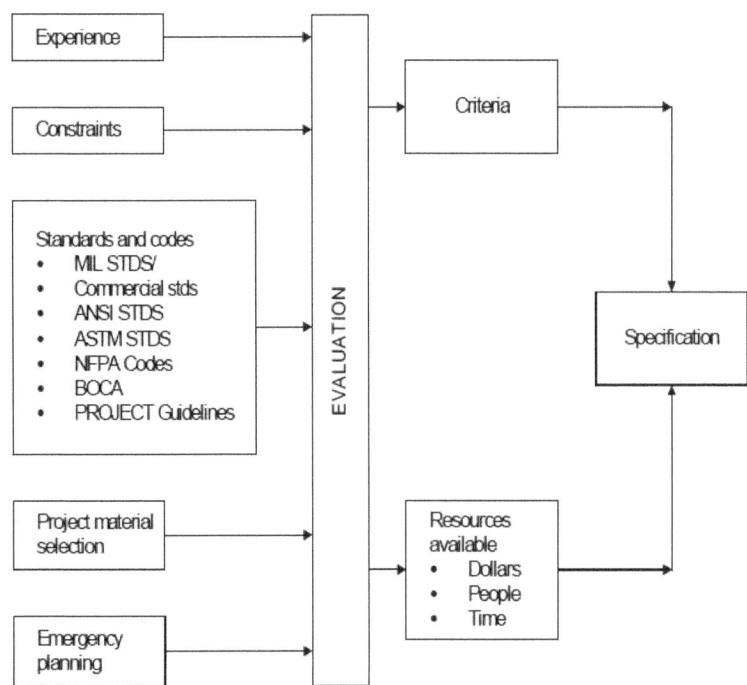

Figure 8: Safety and Security Specification Development Inputs

Safety and security design criteria may be consolidated into a single manual or list for the project, or referenced as part of project development for each certifiable element. A representative process for incorporating these criteria into the project design process is illustrated graphically in Figure 9 below:

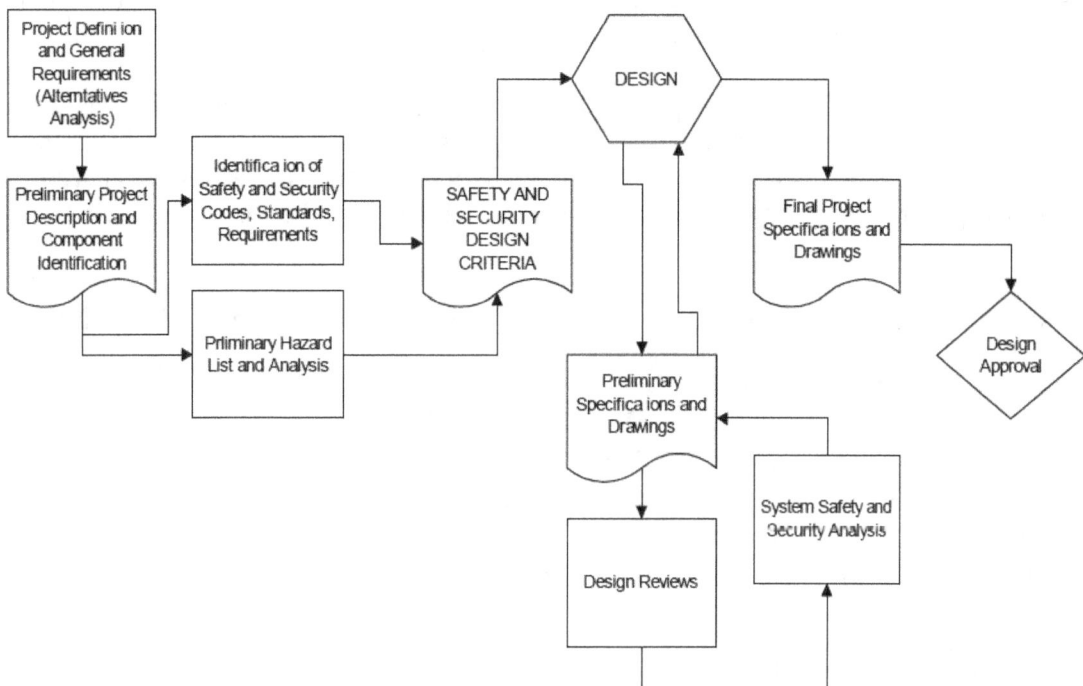

Figure 9: Safety and Security Design Criteria and Project Specification

RESOURCES: FTA's *Hazard Analysis Guidelines for Transit Projects* and APTA's *Manual for the Development of Rail Transit System Security Program Plans* both provide additional information on the role and management of analysis in project design. These documents are available for download on FTA's web site: www.fta.dot.gov (click on "Safety and Security") and APTA's web site: www.apta.com.

Appendices B and C also contain useful references and sample codes for development of safety and security design criteria.

STEP 3: Develop and Complete Design Criteria Conformance Checklist

During design, the project team may begin identifying criteria requirements for certifiable elements and items. This process involves the creation of a checklist for each certifiable element to record requirements generated from safety and security design criteria. These checklists – referred to as *Design Criteria Conformance Checklists* – provide a format to verify compliance with identified safety and security requirements.

In the certification process, contract specifications, design criteria, applicable codes, and industry standards may constitute this verification. For example, some of the requirements in contract specifications may be used as verification, such as maintenance manuals, subsystem hazard analysis, and factory test reports. Other requirements may not take the form of specific deliverable documents, but require verification.

Following initial development, the Design Criteria Conformance Checklist is submitted to the appropriate personnel for review and comment. A sample Design Criteria Conformance Checklist is provided in Figure 10.

During development of these checklists, it may also be necessary for the project team to reference safety and security requirements for use in design reviews and during inspections or tests. Identification of these activities provides an opportunity for the entire project team to assess the status of the SSC program through the following activities:

- Briefings on major safety and security program milestones, including hazard identification and analysis, vulnerability assessments, required test, inspections and procedures, and special issues not yet resolved

- Identification of subsystem, component, and software safety activities as well as integrated system level activities (i.e., design analyses, tests, and demonstrations) applicable to the SSC program but specified as tasks for which other transit agency or contractor personnel or functions are responsible

- Delivery of reports and analyses documenting the consequences of specific project decisions for safety and security levels, including recommendations

- Identification or presentation of evaluation results relating to requests for deviation from approved baseline designs, procedures, or practices

- Scheduling coordination and group priority setting for safety activities to be addressed in the next project phase

- Status of compliance with identified regulations.

Finally, during this phase of the safety certification process, it is important to identify the process to be used for the management and tracking of "open items." The term "open items" refers to items that have not been verified for conformance with design requirements, as well as unresolved safety or security issues. As the project proceeds through design to construction to start-up, reviews are often performed to verify that change proposals and deviations from the approved baseline design do not degrade the level of safety and security of the system to unacceptable levels. "Open items" are often addressed during these reviews.

Design Verification for Safety and Security Certifiable Items

Element:_____   Page_____ of _____
Sub-Element:_____   Prepared by:_____
Revision:_____   Date:_____
Contract Number:

Status	Means of Verification - Design
C = Compliance	S = Submittal
N = Noncompliance	D = Design
P = Partial Compliance	

Item No.	Description	Safety Design Criteria	Design Cross References	Design Verification			Means of Verification
				Status	Initial	Date	

Name   Signature   Date

Organization

NOTES/EXCEPTIONS:

Figure 10: Design Criteria Conformance Checklist

STEP 4: Perform Construction Specification Conformance

The construction specification conformance process is used to verify that the as-built facilities and systems incorporate the safety and security-related requirements identified in the specifications and other contract documents, including approved changes since the final design.

This checklist should be viewed as the "other half" of the Design Criteria Conformance Checklist, because it (1) identifies the tests and verification methods necessary to ensure that the as-built configuration contains the safety-related requirements identified in the applicable specifications and other contract documents, and (2) provides documentation that the delivered project meets these requirements. The *Specification Conformance Checklist* is the "work horse" of the SSC process.

Once the checklist format is completed, verified checklists are forwarded to appropriate staff for review and comment. Documentation supporting verification of the safety requirement should be available for review by the project team. For facilities and systems, certifications, inspector reports, job photos, or other evidence may be submitted as documentation. Any contractor submittal used for verification needs to be approved, typically by the resident engineer.

Safety and security requirements not verified by available documentation or demonstration should be tracked to resolution. As mentioned in Step 3, the management or resolution of open items should result through project team's use of the Specification Conformance Checklist. This checklist provides those responsible for decision-making a tool to review the status of open items resulting from deviations to the approved design, work-arounds, change orders, and other temporary measures.

Three Specification Conformance Checklists, (two with sample entries), are presented below. Figure 11 identifies an excerpt from a specification checklist to demonstrate the types of issues typically encountered for an at-grade light rail station. Figure 12 provides sample documentation of non-compliance regarding safety and security requirements for right-of-way signage. Figure 13 provides a sample checklist that can be used to document both design and construction conformance. Directions for completing this form are provided in Appendix D. This type of checklist is easily incorporated into an automated information system, to support SSC program tracking and documentation requirements.

Some transit agencies may choose to compile supporting verification documentation for each certifiable element in separate notebooks. Some guidelines that may be used in the verification process include the following:

1. Use documentation that directly and succinctly verifies the safety and/or security requirement
2. Exclude irrelevant or redundant information
3. For large contract submittals, include representative information only
4. Highlight specific detail from approved contractor submittals and other verification documentation to aid the review process

		Contract # C-60					

Certifiable Element: E-1		Subsystem: Station / At-Grade					
No.	**Safety Requirement**	**Standard/ Source**	**Compliance: Specs, As-Built Dwgs;Pg#**	**Y**	**N**	**N/A**	**Means of Verification/ Remarks**
Note: NFPA = National Fire Protection Association, UFC = Uniform Fire Code							
1	Construction Material (Type I or II)	NFPA 130/2-2, UFC-Chap. 6, *Design Criteria Manual*, Chap. 8	Specs 03462, 05130, 05300, 07410	X			Visual Verification
2	Electrical Requirements - General	NFPA 70, NFPA 130/2-4.1, *Design Criteria Manual* 28	Specs 16001, 16030, 16111, 16120, 16130, 16490, 16450, 16470, 16500, EC1-0003-0005, pgs 659-661	X			Visual Verification
3	Identification of Breakers	*Design Criteria Manual* 28.7.2, NFPA 70	Specs 16040, 16470 EC1-0003-0005, pgs 659-661	X			Visual Verification
4	Passenger Egress	NFPA 130/2-5 and Appendix C	Dwg AC2-0004, pg 585	X			Visual Verification
5	Passenger Access	*Design Criteria Manual* 19.2.2	Dwg AC2-0004, pg 585	X			Visual Verification
6	Emergency Lighting	*Design Criteria Manual* 26.5.4, NFPA 130/2-6	Dwg AC2-0004, pg 585			X	
7	Automatic Fire Detection	*Design Criteria Manual* 27.4, NFPA 130/2-7.1.5	N/A			X	
	Emergency Communication	NFPA 130/2-7.2; 3.1.5 and 8-7	AC2-0005-0007, pgs 586-588; EC2-0003-0005, pgs 659-661	X			Pay phones need to be connected for emergency communication devices. Both phones working 9/21/01 – Close.

Figure 11: Sample Specification Conformance Checklist

Certifiable Element:	E-4
Contract:	Contract-01
Revision Date:	03-27-2002
Prepared By:	Joe Safety

**Light Rail Transit
LRT Buildout Phase 1
Safety/Security Certification Checklist**

Subsystem: Trainway - Surface				Design Phase Certified – 8/24/00				Construction / Installation / Test SSCRT Certified			
Item	Safety Requirement	Standard / Source	Compliance, Specifications, or Drawings	Remarks	Status			Remarks (Date Verified)	Status		
					Yes	No	N/A		Yes	No	N/A
1	ROW Safety / Warning Signage	NFPA 130/3-1.3	Conformed Spec 2847, Conformed Dwg(s) RC9-4001 to 4007 pp. 93-99		X					X	
										X	
										X	
								station at-grade crossings.		X	
								G. Sign removed on track 2 side at 952+00, station.		X	

Figure 12: Sample Specification Conformance Checklist with Non-compliance

Status	Means of Verification - Design	Means of Verification - Construction
C = Compliance	**S = Submittal**	**M = Measurement**
N = Noncompliance	**D = Design**	**T = Test**
P = Partial Compliance		**V = Visual Inspection**

Certifiable Element:
Checklist Type: Master: Sub:
Sub-Element:_____
Contract Number:
Safety: Security:
Specification/Drawing Reference:_____
Document Control Number:_____
Revision:

NOTES OR RESTRICTIONS:

Item No.	Description	Design Cross Reference	Design Verification				Construction Verification			
			Status	Initial	Date	Means of Verification	Status	Initial	Date	Means of Verification

FINAL DESIGN VERIFICATION
Name and Organization:_____
Date: _____
Approved By: _____
Date: _____

FINAL CONSTRUCTION VERIFICATION
Name and Organization:_____
Date:_____
Approved By:_____
Date:_____

Figure 13: Sample Design and Construction Conformance Checklist with Directions

STEP 5: Identify Additional Safety and Security Test Requirements

Contractor and integrated testing requirements should be reviewed for safety and security considerations. Contractor testing, as required by the contract specifications, verifies the functionality of the involved system or equipment. Integrated testing verifies the functional interface between different equipment or systems. Both contractor and integrated testing are subject to certification. Certification of contractor testing may be verified in the Specification Conformance Checklist, or combined with integrated testing in a test program certification or by other acceptable means.

The need for additional tests, however, may arise for various reasons throughout the project. To request and record the performance of additional tests, the project team may prepare a formal Test Description Sheet and submit it to the appropriate organizational unit managing the Test Program Plan. A sample Test Description Sheet follows:

REQUIRED SAFETY AND SECURITY TEST DESCRIPTION SHEET		
Test Name:		
Test Procedure:		
Contracts Involved:		
Test Objectives:		
Test Description:		
Test Prerequisites:		
Resources Required	**Personnel:**	
	Equipment:	
	Facilities:	
Time Required:		

Figure 14: Required Test Description Sheet

STEP 6: Perform Testing and Validation in Support of the SSC Program

From the initial stages of the construction development phase, test reports and other documentation will be submitted to the agency as a result of Design Qualification Tests (Factory); Production Verification Tests (Factory); Construction Inspection Tests; and Installation Verification Tests (QA/QC). Safety/security-related test results should be documented, as appropriate, in the Specification Conformance Checklist.

Appropriate documentation supporting verification of the safety and security requirements should be submitted or available for review by the project team with its location clearly identified. The SSC should identify responsibilities for control and lifecycle of all certification documentation. Those personnel responsible for safety and security certification should work closely with all involved in this process to achieve full access to the testing and results. This process is illustrated below:

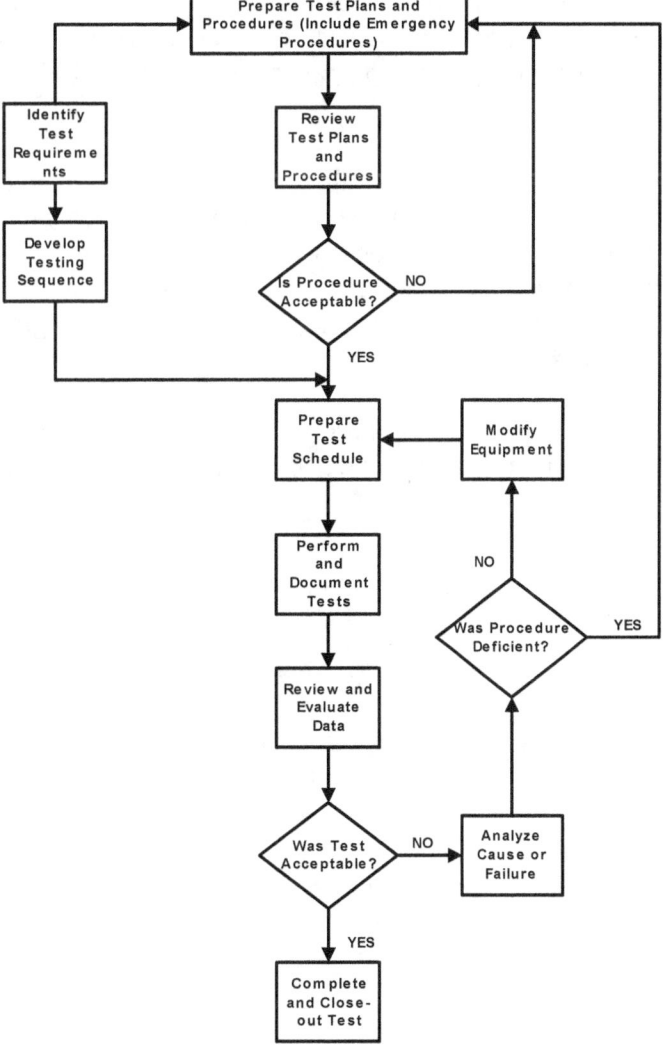

Figure 15: Test Program Planning Process

STEP 7: Manage Integrated Tests for the SSC Program

Integrated tests are any tests or series of tests, which require the interface of more than one element and are designed to verify the integration and compatibility between system elements. Pre-operations tests are those tests that require acceptance of all systems and are designed to verify the functional capability and readiness of the system as a whole. These tests are not necessarily required by contract specification, but are required as part of the test program plan to ensure that all systems are functioning safely prior to the system being placed into operation. Test result reports form the basis for meeting the safety requirements.

Prior to developing a plan for integrated testing, transit agencies typically assess both the scope of the project related to existing or planned operations and the initial safety and security requirements. In specifying the tests, transit agencies often identify a minimum level of safety and security conformance that should be met, as well as the measurables used to assess this conformance. This minimum level varies from project to project, and is dependent upon the level of integration and the nature of the tests to be performed. It is important to note that transit agencies should review test procedures, themselves, for potential hazards. The transit agency may also want to develop emergency plans to prepare for a potential critical or catastrophic test failure.

The transit agency may assign a "System Integration Manager" or equivalent personnel to be responsible for test management. This manager is often supported in test planning, test procedure development and test performance by Operations, Maintenance and the Safety and Security Review Committee. The organizational group designated to manage start-up activities also receives support from these groups in scheduling facility access and arranging for human resources to conduct and witness the test.

Copies of all applicable tests and inspection reports should become part, of or be referenced in, the formal SSC files. A sample integrated test description sheet is provided below.

SYSTEM INTEGRATION TESTING TEST DESCRIPTION SHEET	
Test Name:	LRV Clearance Test
Test Procedure:	SI – 101
Contracts Involved:	C510 - Civil, Track and Landscaping C540 - Stations and Park and Ride S510 - OCS and LRT Signal System
Test Objectives:	Verify that there is adequate clearance between the LRV and the equipment and facilities along the mainline.
Test Description:	Tow a vehicle, equipped with foam extenders to represent the Dynamic envelope, over the mainline right-of-way with the pantograph retracted Confirm clearances are as specified. Test will be repeated when Low Floor Vehicles are available.
Test Prerequisites:	Equipment and facilities installed along mainline right-of-way.
Resources Required — **Personnel:**	Test Coordinator Test Controller Rail Activation Maintenance Engineering CM Representative Vehicle Operator
Equipment:	Hi-Rail Vehicle Mover Light Rail Vehicle LRV Foam Extenders Measuring Tape Radios (4)
Facilities:	Both mainline tracks
Time Required:	8 to 12 hours

Figure 16: Sample Integrated Testing Sheet

STEP 8: Manage "Open Items" in the SSC Program

As the certification proceeds, open items will be identified and will need to be managed. During pre-revenue testing and start-up activities, requests for work-arounds and temporary permits of occupancy/notices will be made. The SSC program must have the tools available to ensure that the safety and security designed into the system are realized in the delivered, tested, and validated project.

A *Safety Critical Items List* (SCIL) can be used to track the status and/or resolution of those open items identified with the potential to result in harm. Depending on definitions used for the project, these items may represent catastrophic and critical hazards and vulnerabilities, defined as Category I and Category II hazards using Checklist Number 7 of the American Public Transportation Association's *Manual for the Development of Rail Transit System Safety Program Plans* and also referenced in the FTA *Hazard Analysis Guidelines*. Category I and II hazards may require additional analysis to be performed to ensure that mitigation measures adopted to eliminate or minimize their risk will be effective in doing so before revenue operations can commence.

The SCIL, or other log, can also support tracking of exceptions or restrictions in those situations when a safety certifiable element/item cannot meet design specification with the initiation of revenue service. These exceptions must be accompanied by acceptable operational work-arounds, if the item is critical for the commencement of revenue operations. The work-arounds should proscribe operational policies and procedures that ensure safe system operations, even though certification requirements are not completed. It is important that safety, security, and operations representatives and the project manager are equally aware of the accepted measures and the item is tracked to resolution (it should be noted that in some cases accepted measures may be permanent). The figure below presents a sample close-out report for significant items.

STATUS REPORT FOR CLOSE-OUT				
Item No.	System Element:	Sub-system:	Reference Information:	Date:
Description of Condition:		Required Controls:		
Status:		Responsibility:		Approved:
		Name:	Department:	

Figure 17: Sample Close-out Report

STEP 9: Verify Operational Readiness

Operational readiness includes activities to verify the following:

- Applicable operations, maintenance, and emergency rules, procedures, and plans have been developed, reviewed, and implemented

- Manuals, showing how to operate and maintain systems equipment and facilities, have been developed, reviewed, approved, and accepted by the project team

- Safety/security-related training for operations and maintenance personnel has been developed, performed, and successfully completed by all personnel as required

- Emergency training has been developed, performed, and successfully completed by all personnel as required, including public safety personnel (if appropriate)

- Emergency drills and training have been conducted with outside agencies
  - To familiarize and train response personnel in emergency procedures
  - To evaluate response procedures
  - To identify improvements to response procedures before a real emergency occurs
  - To maintain an adequate level of preparation for a possible emergency.

During the pre-operations phase of the system, the procedures and plans are tested for effectiveness under simulated operating conditions for normal, abnormal, and emergency situations. Verification for these activities often includes signatures by the appropriate officials or employees on all procedures, rulebooks, and training necessary to support operation and maintenance of the system. The operating and maintenance procedures and plans are judged as meeting the verification requirements or are recommended for modification.

In addition, during this period, the project team should conduct a final "walk-through inspection" of completed facilities and systems.

STEP 10: Conduct Final Determination of Project Readiness and Issue Safety and Security Certification

Before revenue service begins, prior to completing its formal certification, the project team and supporting committees should review all safety and security certification documentation to determine if any outstanding items remain.

Approval of certifiable elements occurs when work has been completed in conformance with criteria and hazards have been reduced to an acceptable level. Any remaining work-arounds affecting a certifiable element require a hazard management plan to be initiated that will analyze the hazard and control the risk to an acceptable level for a defined period of time. The hazard management plan must include any Category I and II hazards to ensure that they have been resolved or controlled to an acceptable level prior to entering revenue service.

When a certifiable element is ready for certification, the Safety and Security Review Committee (or other designated authority) should evaluate the evidence, along with any restrictions and recommendations, and prepare a "Certificate of Conformance" package.

In the event that an "Interim Request for Certificate" has been put forward, any subsequent certification should identify restrictions that remain on system elements under the request. These restrictions should be communicated to all affected departments in writing, and the residual risk accepted should be accepted by the designated and appropriate authority within the agency.

If the Safety and Security Review Committee determines that the requirements have not been met, then it has the responsibility and authority to recommend to the Chief Executive Officer that operation of the system be delayed until the issue is resolved.

Upon completion of all project Certificates of Conformance (with specific restrictions as applicable), a Final Project Safety and Security Certificate is prepared, signed and transmitted to the transit agency executive management for formal approval. A sample certification is presented in Figure 18 below.

SAFETY AND SECURITY CERTIFICATION PROGRAM
PROJECT SAFETY AND SECURITY CERTIFICATE
RESTRICTIONS:
The **PROJECT SAFETY AND SECURITY CERTIFICATE** indicates that all safety and security requirements have been successfully completed and the project is certified for revenue service, but with any noted restrictions.
_____   _____ Prepared by and Date   Approved by and Date

Figure 18: Project Safety and Security Certificate

Prior to revenue operations, or shortly after the initiation of revenue service, the project team will prepare a Safety and Security Certification Verification Report. This report summarizes the readiness of the project for revenue service by addressing the following elements:

- Executive Summary regarding Status of SSC and Restrictions

- Description of Activities Performed for SSC
    - Design and Construction Checklists
    - Integrated Testing
    - Emergency Drills
    - Contractual Operations and Maintenance Manuals
    - Fire/Life Safety Training
    - Operations and Maintenance Training

- Description of Current Certification Status
    - Signed Certificates of Conformance
    - Final Project Safety and Security Certificate

- Recommendation of Actions Required to Mitigate or Minimize the Consequences of the Remaining Restrictions

- Schedule for Eliminating Restrictions

In some states, the Verification Report must be submitted to the State Safety Oversight Agency.

APPENDIX A: Life Cycle Definitions

Planning – begins with research conducted into the feasibility of a project and concludes with the creation of a concept and the decision to develop a preliminary design. This phase is managed through the local transportation planning function and proceeds through alternative analysis and special research, environmental impact assessments, corridor analyses, and major investment studies. It concludes with the formal adoption of a locally preferred alternative and the request to enter Preliminary Engineering.

Preliminary Engineering (PE) -- takes the project from the planning stage to a level of design that allows a more accurate estimate of project costs and impacts. The results of PE provide the basis for subsequent funding and implementation decisions. A major objective of PE is to investigate the merits of all configurations and designs. These investigations require in-depth analysis of all components, their interrelationships, and their costs. Environmental reviews are also performed.

Final Design (FD) – takes the formalized concept and engineering development and finalizes them in the plans, specifications, and bid documents required for awarding the individual construction and equipment fabrication and installation contracts.

Construction (CON) – begins with the development, fabrication, or construction of the engineered design for the selected alternative and concludes with the delivery of the completed project. This phase include the inspection, review, and checkout of the delivered project and concludes with the determination that the delivered project meets the engineering specification.

Integrated Testing (INT-TEST) – begins with activities to identify, plan and conduct tests to evaluate integration of the delivered and accepted project into planned revenue operations. This phase concludes with verified documentation of compatibility between system elements.

Pre-revenue (Interim) Operations (PRE-REV) – begins with the identification and performance of tests, drills, exercises, and audits designed to verify the functional capability and readiness of the system as a whole, and concludes with verified documentation of readiness for revenue operations.

Operations (OPS) – begins with the initiation of the completed project in service and concludes with the determination that the project has fulfilled its service requirements and must be replaced or removed from operations.

APPENDIX B: Useful References

29 CFR 1910.119, "Process Safety Management," Department of Labor, OSHA, U.S. Government Printing Office, July 1992.

American Public Transportation Association. *Manual for the Development of Rail Transit System Safety Program Plans*, 1999.

Boyd, Annabelle, Patricia Maier and James Caton. *Transit Security Handbook*. Washington, D.C.: Federal Transit Administration, 1998.

Boyd, Annabelle and John Sullivan. *Emergency Preparedness for Transit Terrorism*. Transit Cooperative Research Program, Synthesis Number 27, Washington, D.C.: National Academy Press, 1997.

Christensen, Wayne C. and Fred A. Manuele, Editors. *Safety through Design*. NSC Press, ISBN 0-87912-204-8, 1999.

Clarke, Ronald, et al. *Preventing Mass Transit Crimes: Prevention Studies*, Criminal Justice Press, 1996.

Cobb, Renee and Jerome Needles. *Improving Transit Security*. Transit Cooperative Research Program, Synthesis Number 21, Washington, D.C.: National Academy Press, 1997.

Crowe, Timothy D. *Crime Prevention through Environmental Design: Applications of Architectural Design and Space Management Concepts*, Stoneham, MA: Butterworth Press, 1991.

Hammer, Willie. *Product Safety Management and Engineering*. Second Edition, ASSE, ISBN 0-939874-90-3, 1993.

MIL-STD 882-D, "System Safety Program Requirements," February 10, 2000.

MIL-STD 1629A, "Procedures for Performing a Failure Mode, Effects and Criticality Analysis," November 1980.

National Transit Institute. Transit Trainers' Workshop. *Session Workbook: Keeping Operators Safe A Comprehensive Approach*, January 2001.

Policastro, Anthony and Susanna Gordon. *The Use of Technology in Preparing Subway Systems for Chemical/Biological Terrorism*. Washington, D.C.: Department of Energy, May 1999.

Raheja, Dev. *Products Assurance Technologies: Principles and Practice*. New York: McGraw Hill, Inc., 1991.

Roland, Harold E., Moriarty, Brian, *System Safety Engineering and Management*, Second Edition, John Wiley & Sons, Inc., 1990.

Sullivan, John and Henry DeGeneste. *Policing Transportation Facilities*. Springfield, IL: Charles C. Thomas Press, 1994.

System Safety Society, *System Safety Analysis Handbook*, 2nd Edition, System Safety Society, Sterling, VA 1997.

U.S. Department of Defense, Joint Software Safety Committee, *Software System Safety Handbook*, December 1999.

U.S. General Services Administration. *Balancing Security & Openness*. Washington, D.C., November 30, 1999.

U.S. General Services Administration. *Facility Standards for the Public Building Service*. "Chapter 8: Security." Washington, D.C. 2001.

Veteran's Benefits Administration. *Facility Design Guide*. Washington, D.C. 1999.

Vincoli, Jeffrey, *Basic Guide to System Safety*, Van Nostrand Reinhold Press, 1993.

APPENDIX C: Resource Guide

The following organizations provide standards, codes and regulations commonly used to support this activity:

AAR ....Association of American Railroads
APTA .... American Public Transportation Association
AREMA ....American Railway and Engineering and Maintenance-of-Way Association
ASCE ....American Society of Civil Engineers
ASHRAE .... American Society of Heating, Refrigerating, and Air-Conditioning Engineers
ASME .... American Society of Mechanical Engineers
ASTM .... American Society for Testing and Materials
FHWA ....Federal Highway Administration
FRA .... Federal Rail Administration
FTA ....Federal Transit Administration
IEEE ....Institute of Electrical and Electronics Engineers
ISO .... International Standards Organization
NGVC ....Natural Gas Vehicle Coalition
NFPA ....National Fire Protection Association
NHTSA ....National Highway Traffic Safety Administration
SAE ....Society of Automotive Engineers
SDO ....Standards Development Organization
TCRP .... Transit Cooperative Research Program
TSC .... Transit Standards Consortium

Detailed descriptions of hazard analysis methodologies can be found in the **System Safety Society's System Safety Analysis Handbook (1997)** and the **Software System Safety Handbook (1999)**. Both handbooks are available on the System Safety Society Web Page: http://www.system-safety.org

The Transportation Safety Institute (TSI) offers several courses that provide detailed descriptions of the hazard analysis process. Additional information on TSI courses and training calendar is available at www.tsi.dot.gov.

Additional standards are available from the following on-line sites:

RESOURCE: The following websites provide additional information on codes, consensus standards, and regulations applicable to major transit projects:

American Institute of Architects _____ www.aia.org
American National Standards Institute (ANSI) _____ www.ansi.org
American Society of Civil Engineers (ASCE) _____ www.asce.org
Building Officials and Code Administrators International _____ www.bocai.org
Construction Specification Institute (CSI)_____ www.csinet.org
Factory Mutual (FM)_____ www.factorymutual.com
Federal Emergency Management Administration (FEMA)_____www.fema.gov
International Code Council _____ www.intlcode.org
International Conference of Building Officials_____ www.icbo.org
National Fire Protection Association Home Page _____ www.nfpa.org
National Institute of Standards and Technology (NIST) _____ www.nist.gov
Occupational Safety and Health Administration (OSHA) _____ www.osha.gov
Southern Building Code Congress International (SBCCI) _____ www.sbcci.org
Transit Standards Consortium _____ www.tsconsortium.org
Underwriters Laboratories, Inc. (U.L.) _____ www.ul.com

RESOURCE: The following links provide information regarding security training and design standards and recommendations:

National Criminal Justice Reference Service _____ www.ncjrs.org
National Crime Prevention Institute _____ www.louisville.edu/a-s/ja/menu.html
National Crime Prevention Council _____ www.ncpc.org
Transportation Safety Institute _____ www.tsi.dot.gov
Maryland Community Crime Prevention Institute_____ www.dpscs.state.md.us/pct/ccpi/
American Society for Industrial Security _____www.asisonline.org

APPENDIX D: Sample Design and Construction Specification Conformance Form and Directions

(Form and Directions Begin on Next Page)

Item No.	Safety Design Criteria	Source/ Standard	Design Cross Reference	Design			Means of Verification	Construction			Means of Verification
				Status	Initial	Date		Status	Initial	Date	

Final Design Verification

Name and Organization: _____

Date: _____

Approved by: _____

Date: _____

Final Construction Verification

Name and Organization: _____

Date: _____

Approved by: _____

Date: _____

NOTES OR RESTRICTIONS:

Certifiable Element: _____

Checklist Type: Master: _____ Sub: _____

Sub-Element: _____

Contract Number: _____ Security: _____

Safety: _____

Specification/Drawing Reference: _____

Document Control Number: _____

Revision: _____

Status	Means of Verification – Design	Means of Verification – Construction
C = Compliance	S = Submittal	M = Measurement
N = Noncompliance	D = Design	T = Test
P = Partial Compliance		V = Visual Inspection

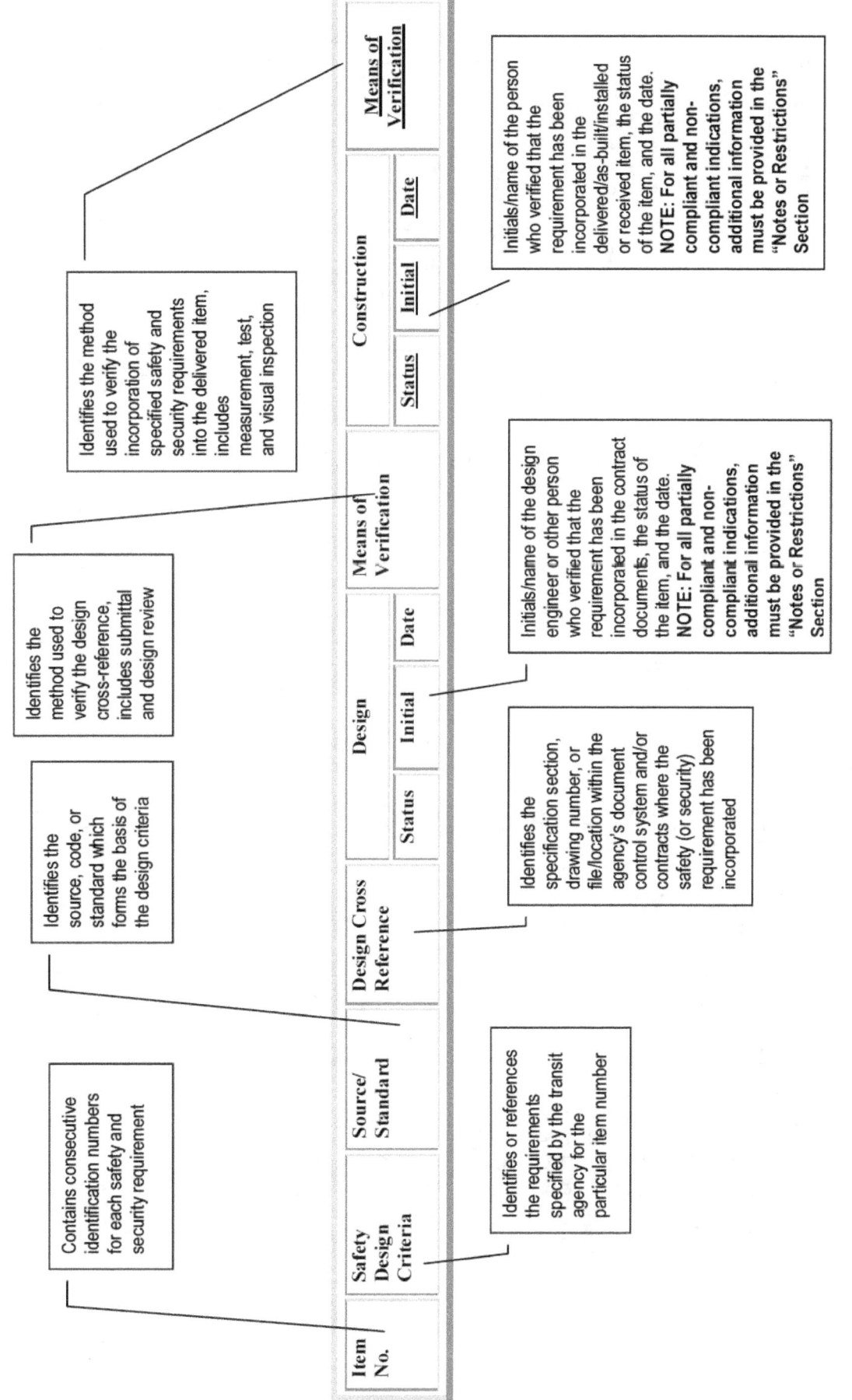

Item No.	Safety Design Criteria	Source/ Standard	Design Cross Reference	Design			Construction		
				Status	Initial	Date	Means of Verification	Status	Initial	Date	Means of Verification

Contains consecutive identification numbers for each safety and security requirement

Identifies or references the requirements specified by the transit agency for the particular item number

Identifies the source, code, or standard which forms the basis of the design criteria

Identifies the specification section, drawing number, or file/location within the agency's document control system and/or contracts where the safety (or security) requirement has been incorporated

Identifies the method used to verify the design cross-reference, includes submittal and design review

Initials/name of the design engineer or other person who verified that the requirement has been incorporated in the contract documents, the status of the item, and the date. **NOTE: For all partially compliant and non-compliant indications, additional information must be provided in the "Notes or Restrictions" Section**

Identifies the method used to verify the incorporation of specified safety and security requirements into the delivered item, includes measurement, test, and visual inspection

Initials/name of the person who verified that the requirement has been incorporated in the delivered/as-built/installed or received item, the status of the item, and the date. **NOTE: For all partially compliant and non-compliant indications, additional information must be provided in the "Notes or Restrictions" Section**

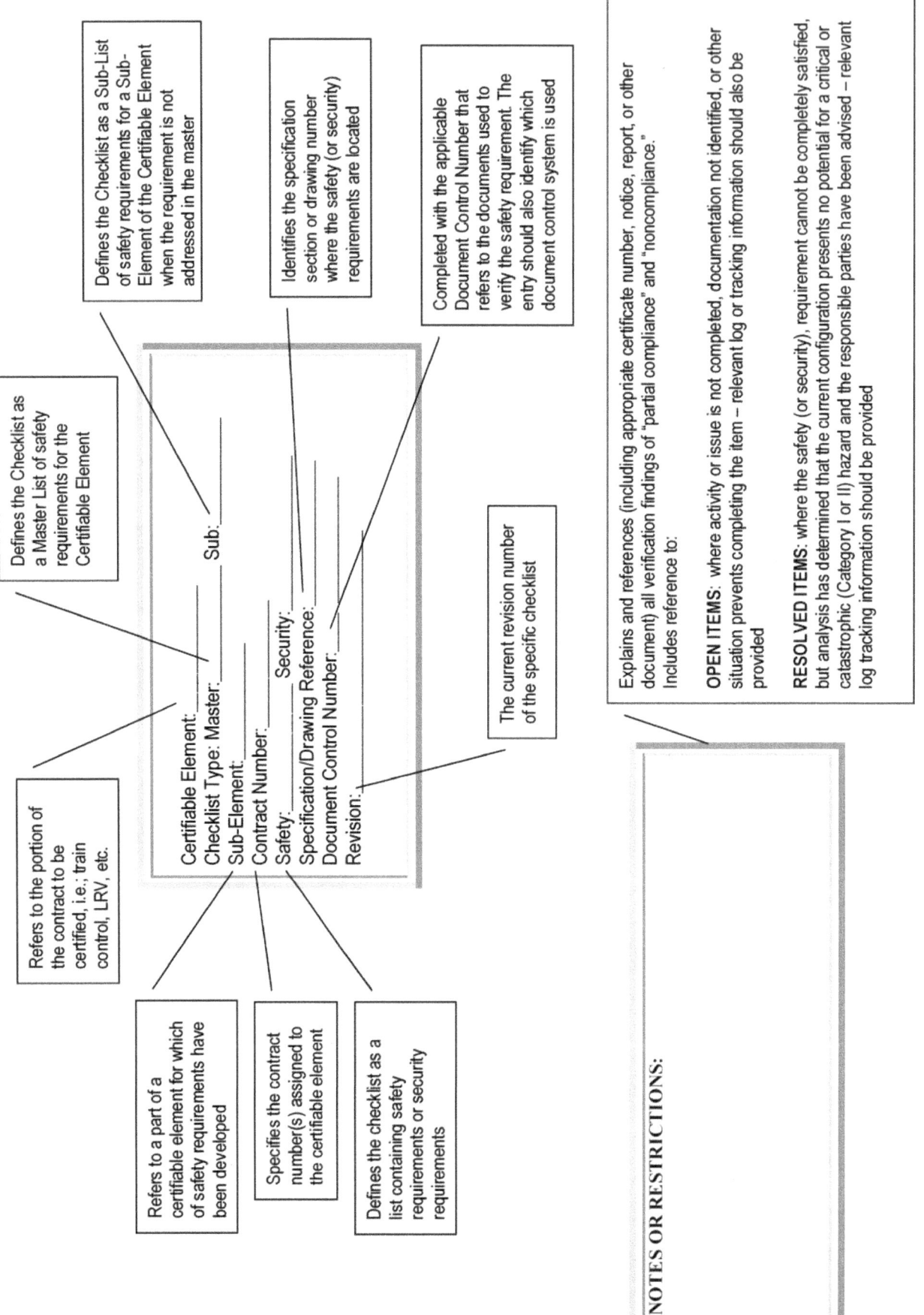

Defines the Checklist as a Sub-List of safety requirements for a Sub-Element of the Certifiable Element when the requirement is not addressed in the master

Identifies the specification section or drawing number where the safety (or security) requirements are located

Completed with the applicable Document Control Number that refers to the documents used to verify the safety requirement. The entry should also identify which document control system is used

Defines the Checklist as a Master List of safety requirements for the Certifiable Element

Refers to the portion of the contract to be certified, i.e.; train control, LRV, etc.

The current revision number of the specific checklist

Certifiable Element:
Checklist Type: Master:_____ Sub:_____
Sub-Element:
Contract Number:_____ Security:_____
Safety:_____ Specification/Drawing Reference:_____
Document Control Number:_____
Revision:_____

Refers to a part of a certifiable element for which of safety requirements have been developed

Specifies the contract number(s) assigned to the certifiable element

Defines the checklist as a list containing safety requirements or security requirements

Explains and references (including appropriate certificate number, notice, report, or other document) all verification findings of "partial compliance" and "noncompliance."
Includes reference to:

OPEN ITEMS: where activity or issue is not completed, documentation not identified, or other situation prevents completing the item – relevant log or tracking information should also be provided

RESOLVED ITEMS: where the safety (or security), requirement cannot be completely satisfied, but analysis has determined that the current configuration presents no potential for a critical or catastrophic (Category I or II) hazard and the responsible parties have been advised – relevant log tracking information should be provided

NOTES OR RESTRICTIONS:

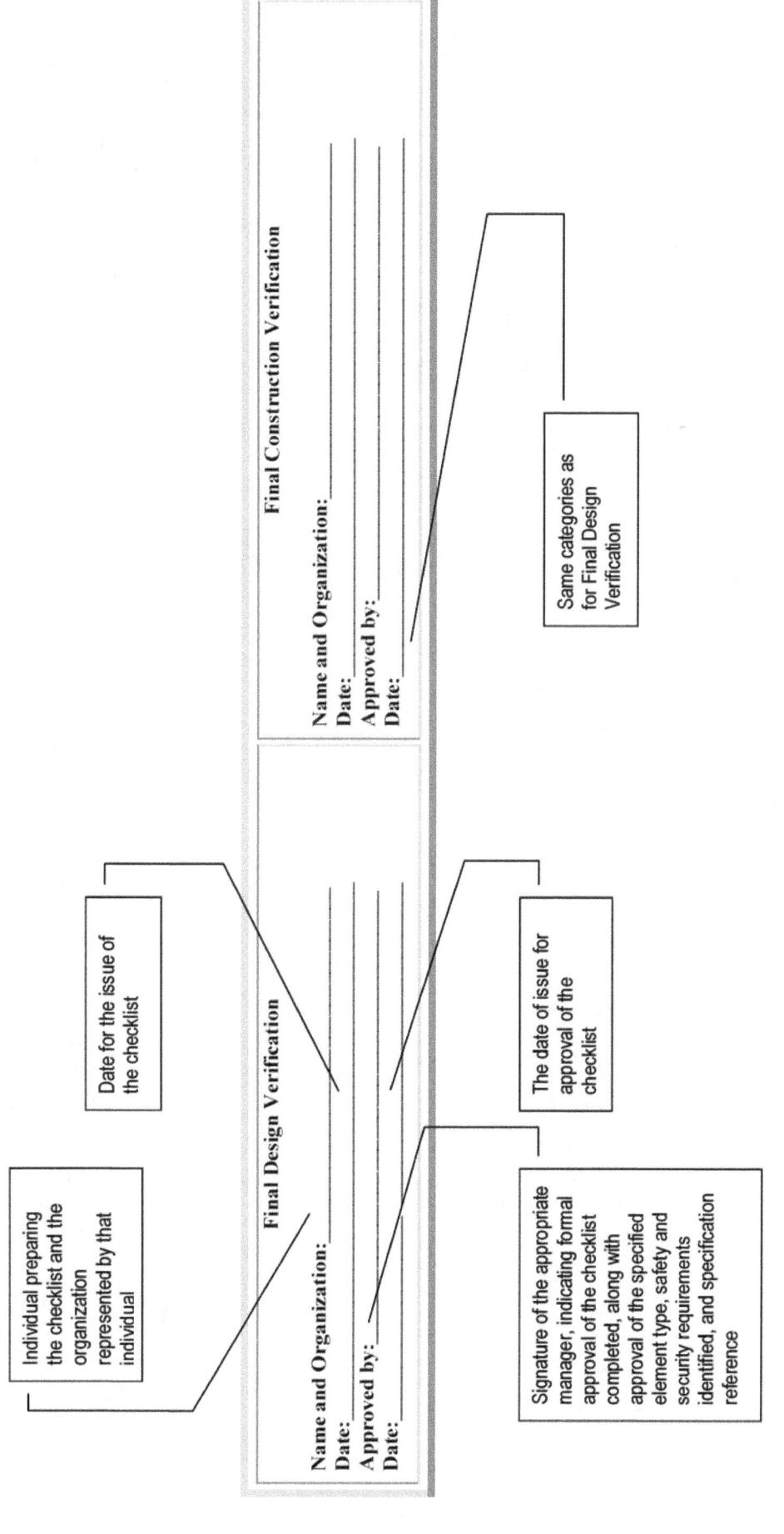

Final Construction Verification

Name and Organization: _____
Date: _____
Approved by: _____
Date: _____

Same categories as for Final Design Verification

Final Design Verification

Name and Organization: _____
Date: _____
Approved by: _____
Date: _____

Individual preparing the checklist and the organization represented by that individual

Date for the issue of the checklist

The date of issue for approval of the checklist

Signature of the appropriate manager, indicating formal approval of the checklist completed, along with approval of the specified element type, safety and security requirements identified, and specification reference